MAKING THE GRADE · GRADE 2

EASY POPULAR PIECES FOR YOUNG PIANISTS. SELECTED AND ARRANGED BY LYNDA FRITH

Exclusive distributors:
Music Sales Limited
Newmarket Road, Bury St. Edmunds, Suffolk IP33 3YB.
This book © Copyright 1991 Chester Music
ISBN 0.7119.2527.5
Order No. CH59261
Cover designed by Pemberton & Whitefoord.
Typeset by Capital Setters Limited.
Printed in the United Kingdom by
Creative Print & Design, Heathrow, Middlesex.

Chester Music
(A division of Music Sales Limited)
8/9 Frith Street, London W1V 5TZ.

INTRODUCTION

This collection of 16 popular tunes has been carefully arranged and graded to provide attractive teaching repertoire for young pianists. New concepts and techniques are introduced progressively, and the familiarity of the material will stimulate pupils' enthusiasm and encourage their practice. The standard of the pieces progresses to Associated Board Grade 2.

CONTENTS

0711925275 01 X8

I DON'T KNOW HOW TO LOVE HIM

by Andrew Lloyd Webber

Try to put real expression and feeling into this piece.

Pay attention to the dynamics and to the phrasing in particular.

You will need to get the fingering exactly right to play it smoothly.

TAKE THAT LOOK OFF YOUR FACE

by Andrew Lloyd Webber

Notice how the left hand imitates (copies) the right hand
in the first eight bars. Make sure that your hands play
exactly together in the four-quaver groups in the time bars.

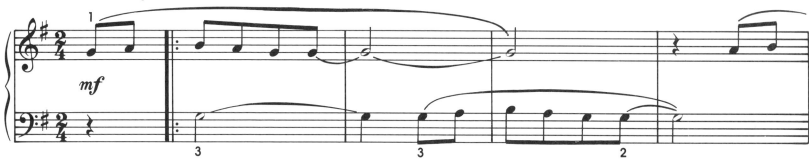

2

AUTUMN FROM 'THE FOUR SEASONS'

by Antonio Vivaldi

This piece was written nearly three hundred years ago, and comes from a group of
four concertos for violin and orchestra which are known as 'The Four Seasons'.
It is one of the best-known pieces in the classical repertoire.

Lively ♩ = 120

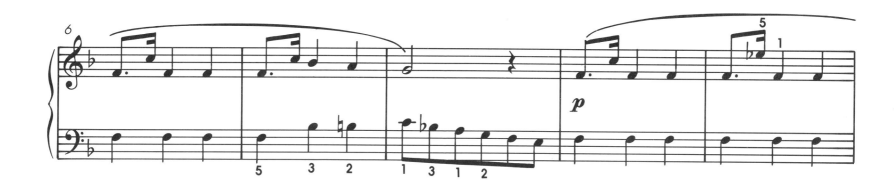

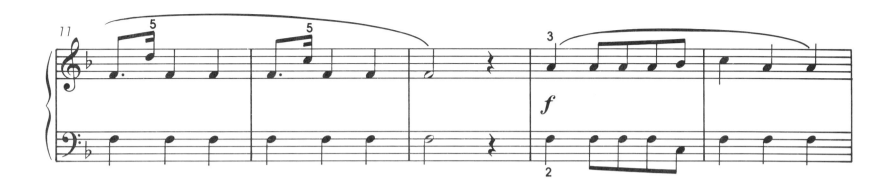

YESTERDAY ONCE MORE

by Richard Carpenter & John Bettis

There are several bars where the left hand has to hold
a semibreve through the bar and also play other notes above it.
Take care to practise these bars carefully.

Moderately ♩=108

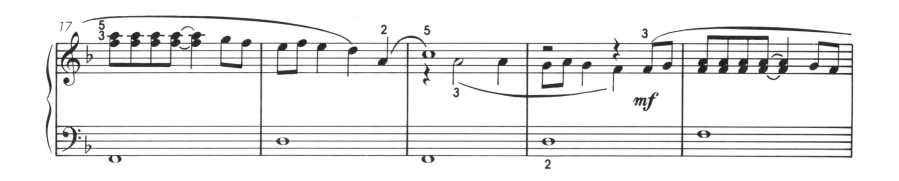

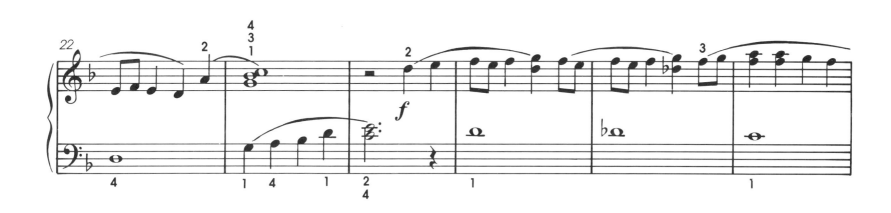

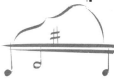

CHIM CHIM CHER-EE

by Richard M. Sherman & Robert B. Sherman

This lively song comes from the musical film 'Mary Poppins'.

Notice how the left hand descends chromatically

(like a chromatic scale, a semitone at a time) in the first part of the piece.

Quite fast ♩. =58

10

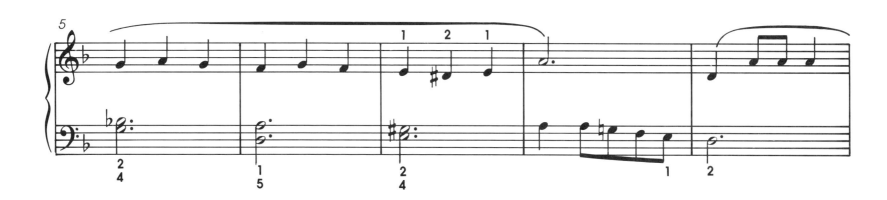

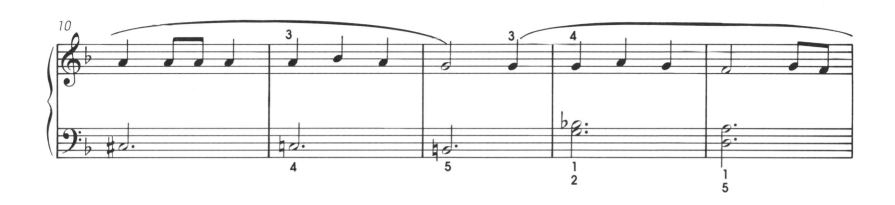

rit.   a tempo

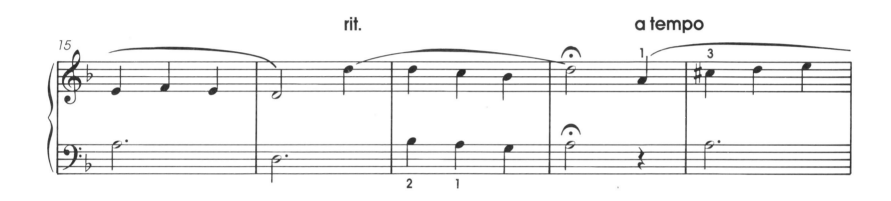

NEIGHBOURS

by Tony Hatch & Jackie Trent

The right-hand fingering in bars four and five is a little tricky,

and well worth some extra practice.

The whole piece should sound smooth and relaxed.

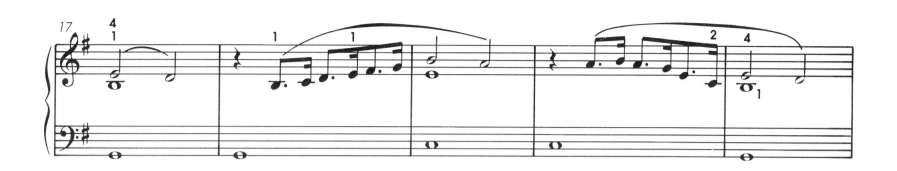

I KNOW HIM SO WELL

by Benny Andersson, Tim Rice & Björn Ulvaeus

Practise each two-bar right hand phrase until it is smooth and even.

From bar eight the left hand becomes more important,

and needs to be heard clearly.

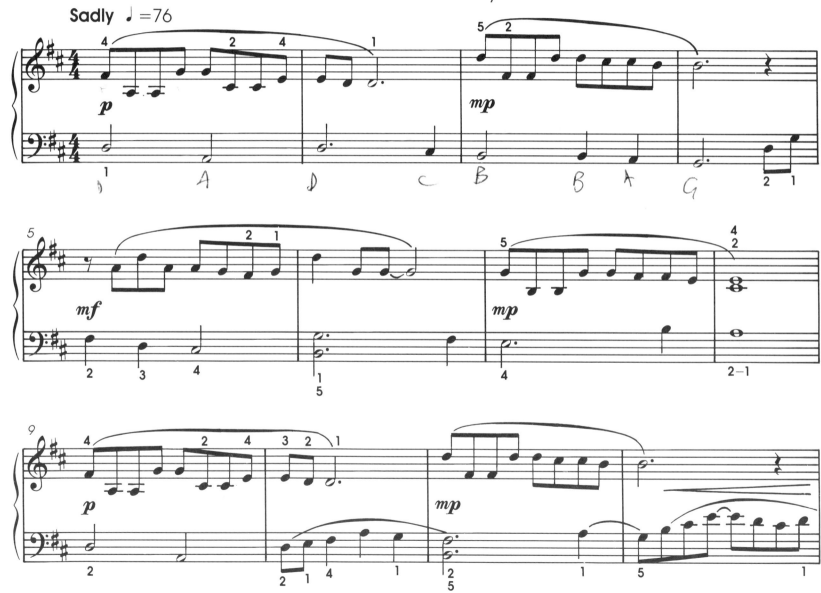

A WINDMILL IN OLD AMSTERDAM

by Ted Dicks & Myles Rudge

There are a lot of extra sharps, flats and naturals on these two pages –
and don't forget that there is an F sharp in the key signature as well!
Read through the piece slowly, hands separately, several times.

With movement ♩ = 144

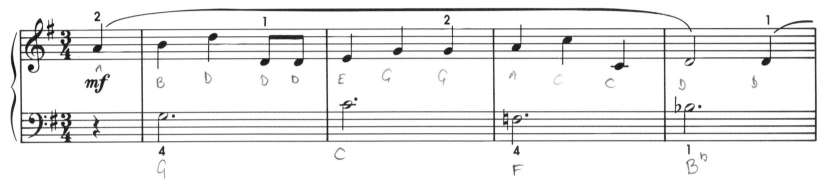

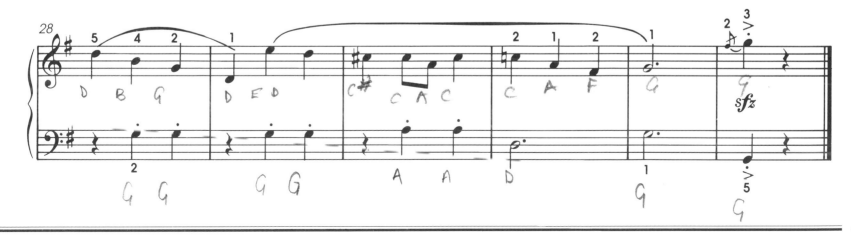

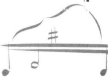

BRIDGE OVER TROUBLED WATER

by Paul Simon

Keep a very steady tempo. If the left hand chord

in the last two bars is too big for you to stretch comfortably,

leave out the Middle C.

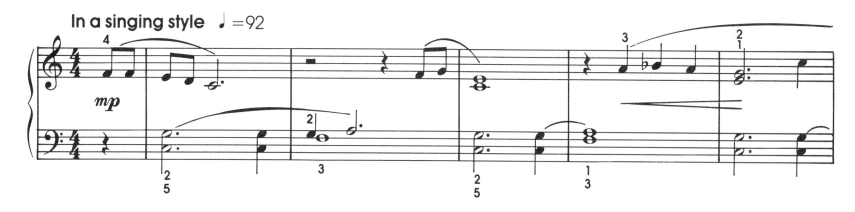

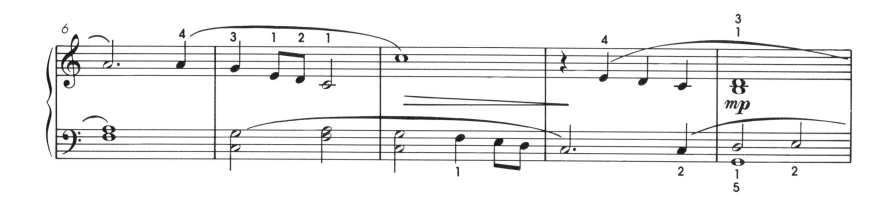

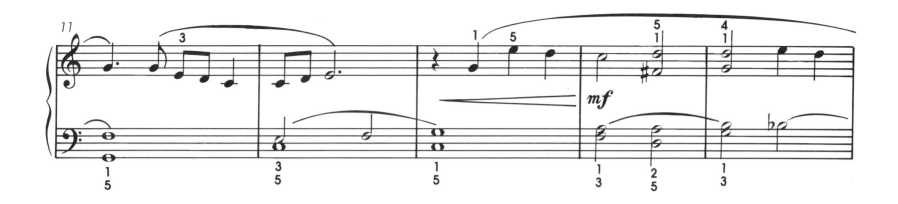

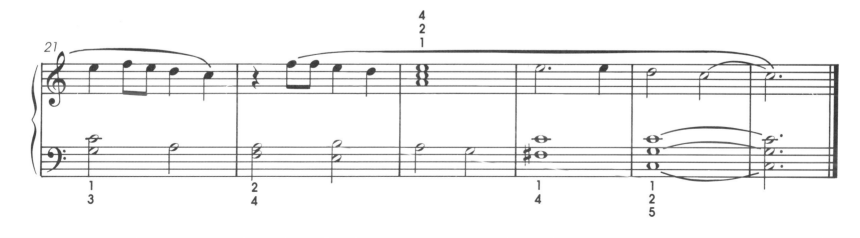

BRIGHT EYES

by Mike Batt

This piece has plenty of dynamic marks in it. Near the end you will see 'sub **mp**'.

This means that you must suddenly play more quietly after the crescendo;

('sub' is short for the Italian word 'subito', meaning 'suddenly').

Sweetly ♩=108

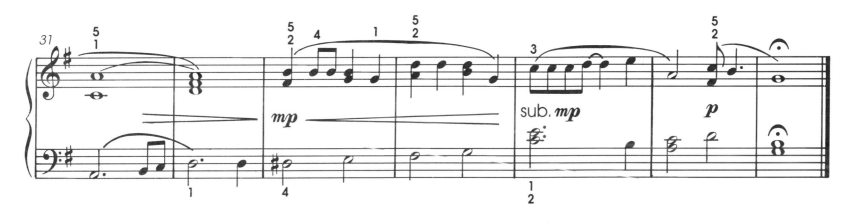

THEME FROM 'SWAN LAKE'

by Peter Tchaikovsky

This is a very exciting and beautiful piece of ballet music.
It is well worth practising hands separately,
being careful to use the correct fingering.

Broadly ♩=100

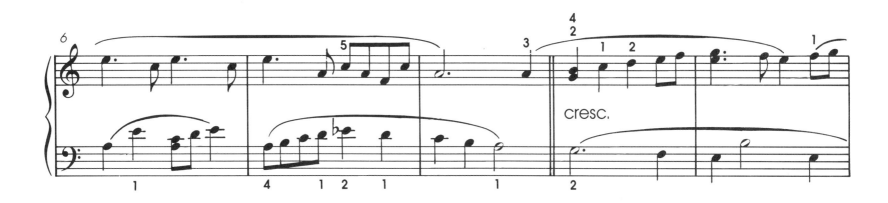

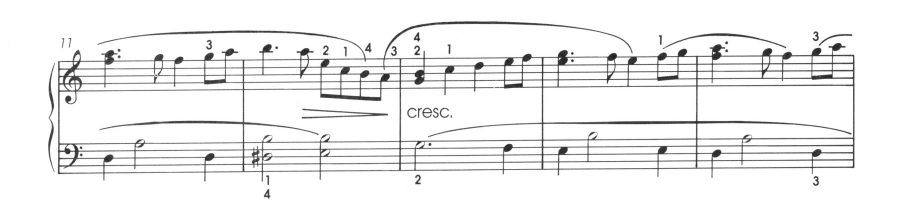

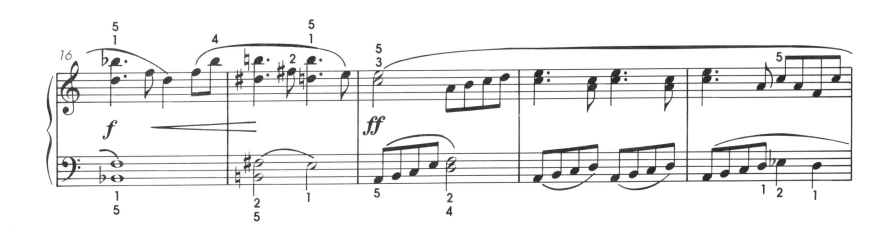

WHERE IS LOVE

by Lionel Bart

Play this song quite slowly and with expression, paying attention
to the dynamics and phrasing. It comes from the musical 'Oliver',
which is based on 'Oliver Twist' by Charles Dickens.

24

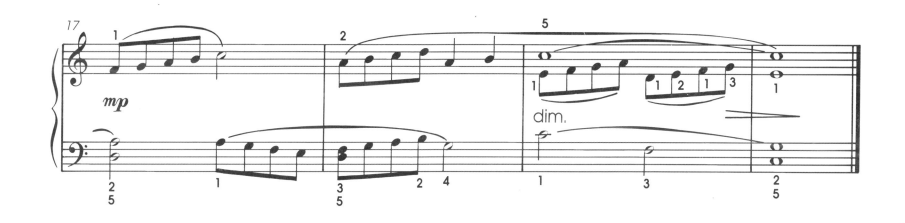

YESTERDAY

by John Lennon & Paul McCartney

Most people's favourite Beatles song, but not the easiest to play.

Practise the right hand in bars two and three carefully,

using the correct fingering in order to play as smoothly as possible.

26

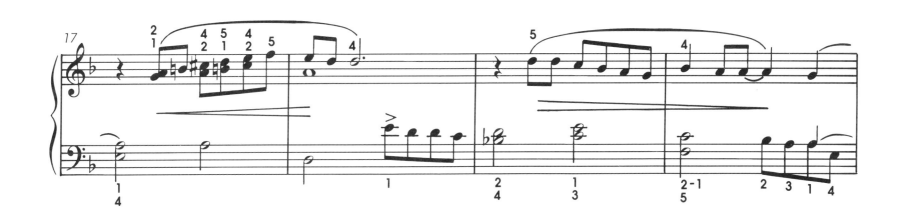

slower

PICK A POCKET OR TWO

by Lionel Bart

This lively and colourful piece from 'Oliver' needs careful attention to
accents and phrasing. Play the staccato notes really short. Notice the G sharps
in the left hand: they need to be 'crushed' into the As and quickly released.

With stealth ♩ = 120

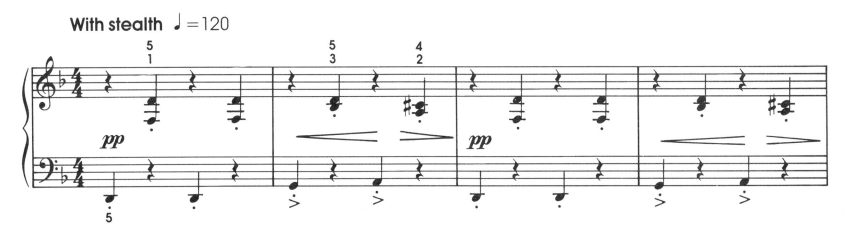

MAPLE LEAF RAG

by Scott Joplin

Look at bars seven and eight before you begin. The right hand starts in the bass clef and moves up to the treble clef, playing the same three notes an octave higher each time. Learn these two bars so that you can look at your fingers when you play them.

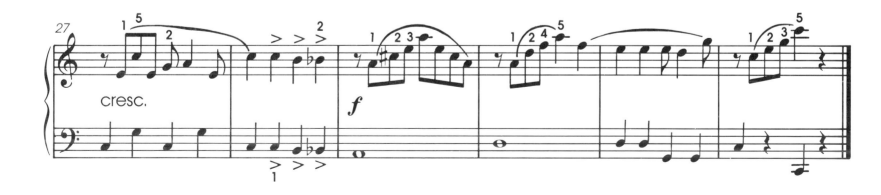

SPRING FROM 'THE FOUR SEASONS'

by Antonio Vivaldi

Both sections are repeated, and should be played loudly (**f**) the first time
and quietly (**p**) the second time. Practise the third phrase in
the right hand carefully, and aim for a good legato.